PERRIER GUIDE TO THE
GREEK MENU

READER'S DIGEST
perrier
GUIDE TO THE
GREEK

Contributor
Claudia Roden

Contributing editor
Lizzie Boyd

PUBLISHED BY
THE READER'S DIGEST
ASSOCIATION LIMITED
LONDON NEW YORK MONTREAL
SYDNEY CAPE TOWN

Perrier/Reader's Digest
Guide to the Greek Menu
was edited and designed by
The Reader's Digest
Association Limited,
London

First Edition Copyright ©
1982 The Reader's Digest
Association Limited,
25 Berkeley Square,
London W1X 6AB
in conjunction with
Aqualac (Spring Waters)
Limited

Copyright © 1982 Reader's
Digest Association Far
East Limited
Philippines Copyright 1982
Reader's Digest
Association Far East
Limited

® READER'S DIGEST is
a registered trademark of
The Reader's Digest
Association, Inc.
of Pleasantville,
New York, U.S.A.

® PERRIER is a
registered trademark of
Source Perrier,
30316 Vergeze, France

Printed in Great Britain

CONTENTS

Foreword by Claudia Roden **6**

Illustrated Guide to Traditional Greek Food:

Starters **10**

Soups **12**

Rice and Pasta Dishes **13**

Savouries and Snacks **14**

Fish and Shellfish **16**

Poultry and Game. **20**

Meat **24**

Vegetables **30**

Salads **34**

Cheeses **36**

Sweets and Pastries · · · · **38**

Fruit **42**

Wines **44**

Coffee and Liqueurs **46**

Glossary of Greek Menu Terms **48**

Acknowledgements **64**

FOREWORD

Our enjoyment of Greek food has much to do with our long-standing love affair with Greece. As the French writer André Malraux once remarked, 'Greece lies at the heart of every man from the West.' The cradle of our civilisation also gave us our standards of taste.

Those who have been intoxicated by the Acropolis and the Parthenon, filled with awe by the landscape of Delphi and with passion at Olympia, and those who have been seduced by Greek hospitality and *joie de vivre*, by the deep blue sea and the magic sunlight are bound to have a special affection for any dish that fills them with nostalgia. Who has not been intrigued by the assortment of stuffed vegetables glimpsed in a tray on a little girl's head as she runs from her house to the taverna in a village of sugar-cake houses? Can the young spring lamb perfumed with pungent *rigani* plucked from the stony hillside ever be forgotten, or red mullet just pulled out of the sea? The memories of aubergines grown fat in the miraculous sunlight, of milk and cheese provided by the goats which eat away the countryside in a concert of tinkling bells, and of honey bees feasting on wild thyme, all these grip our hearts.

Greek food is basically simple and unsophisticated – the staple Mediterranean products of corn, vines and olives, with all sorts of vegetables, provide the everyday dishes cooked in lavish quantities of olive oil. Magnificent grapes, figs, peaches and citrus fruit make puddings superfluous. Cattle breeding has not been successful because of the lack of grazing pastures, but pig and poultry breeding have developed well, and the traditional and favourite meat is that of sheep and goats.

Claudia Roden is the well-known author of the classic A Book of Middle Eastern Food, *as well as* Coffee *and* Picnic. *She also lectures and runs her own cookery school.*

The sea, too, plays its part in the national cuisine; indeed, the sea with its garlands of floating islands *is* Greece. Tunny, red mullet, squid and octopus, prawns and mussels are brought in by trawlers or little boats which go out at night with lanterns and fishing nets.

The style of cooking is Middle Eastern and forms the link in the chain between East and West. Culinary arts reached dazzling heights in Athens in the 5th century AD and had a profound influence on later civilisations. While the Greeks themselves lost the heart and the means for lavish cooking through a long period of decline, the torch of their gastronomy was carried to the ends of the world, even as Greece gained some measure from foreign invasion. Greece has kept the memory of her glorious past and clung to her traditions through the ravages of wars. As a result, eating out is more a convivial affair than a gastronomic event, and the main attraction of pavement cafés and tavernas is the gaiety, the plaintive notes of the *bouzouki* accompanied by love songs and spontaneous dancing.

The most interesting part of a Greek meal is the *Metze*, or appetisers, which accompany drinks, usually beer or *Ouzo*, the fiery anise-flavoured spirit made from grape stems which turns opalescent when water is added, or the pale, resinated *Retsina* wine. *Metze* may be only little bits of cheese, different types of olives, quartered tomatoes, slices of cucumber and spicy garlic sausage. Pistachio nuts, salted almonds, roasted melon seeds and clams are bought from street vendors who sell their wares at café tables. There may also be delicacies such as *Taramasalata* (fish roe dip), mushrooms in oil, pieces of fried liver or octopus, and the famous *Dolmathes* of vine leaves stuffed with rice, pine kernels and raisins.

Formal restaurants may offer a first course of *Pilafi saltsa*, a pasty rice dish, or *Makaronia*, well-done pasta topped with Kefalotiri cheese, or a variety of pies. Apart from the favourite *Avgolemono* soup with eggs and plenty of lemon, there are lovely fish soups to precede the main course, perhaps *Souvlakia* – meat threaded on skewers and cooked over embers – or *Moussaka* of aubergines, minced meat and cheese. The Greeks go to the *Psistarya* to sample spit-roasted lamb or mutton, seasoned only with salt and pepper and accompanied with sliced tomatoes dressed in olive oil, and squares of Feta cheese.

A meal usually ends with fruit. People with a sweet tooth adjourn to a patisserie, the *Zakharoplasteiou*, to satisfy it with round, golden and crisp *Loukoumathes*, yoghourt fritters. They also tuck into a *Baklava, Kataifi* or others of the nutty and syrupy pastries which the Ottoman Turks spread throughout their old far-flung empire, but which, the Greeks claim, are a legacy of their own ancient past.

One local ingredient which is a major factor in the appreciation of Greek food is the traditional hospitality and open-heartedness of the people. Who would not enjoy a bag of newly picked figs presented by a peasant or a bunch of grapes pressed on him by a passer-by? Home-made fruit preserves – compôtes of cherries and strawberries, pumpkin, bitter oranges, apricots, quinces and figs – can never taste as good as when presented in little bowls set on a tray, to be savoured by the spoonful in the most delightful social ritual.

Many dishes are associated with festivals and public holidays. The Feast of St. Basil, on January 1st, is celebrated with a large round brioche, *Vasilopitta*, which contains a good-luck coin. The meatless diet for 'Clean Monday', the first day of Lent, consists of green beans in oil sprinkled with chopped onion, *Taramasalata* and *Dolmathes*, thin flat pitta bread and the ubiquitous *Halva* or syrupy semolina cake. There are many feast days in the Greek Orthodox calendar, all observed in the kitchen, but none as much as Easter. The Good Friday fast is broken with *Mayeritsa*, a rich soup made with lamb's liver and entrails flavoured with dill and enlivened with eggs and lemon juice. On Easter Sunday it is time for red-dyed, hard-boiled eggs, for the sweet plaited bread called *Tsourekia* and for the paschal lambs roasted on spits in gardens and open squares.

In distant lands the Greeks have made many converts to garlic and lemon, *rigani* and mint, to olive oil and Calamata olives as well as to Feta and Halumi cheese. They have taught others the art of making paper-thin pastry and rolling up vine leaves while they dream of the scented air and the brilliant light of the land of the gods. The enterprise of emigrant Greeks in opening cafés, restaurants and grocery stores has brought a knowledge of Greek food to almost every corner of the world.

Claudia Roden

STARTERS

At Greek restaurants in·Britain, a menu will
conform more or less with standard patterns, and an
hors d'oeuvre or soup will precede the main course.
For starters there will be several choices of what in
Greece is called *Mezethakia* – or *mezethes* for short.
They are not so much appetisers as tit-bits to be
eaten with rounds of drinks, at any time of day and
night. At a Greek *taverna*, the host will set down
bowls of nuts and seeds, olives, grapes and pickled
lemons, with spicy dips, plates of fried feta cheese,
radishes and baby turnips.

Mezethakia
APPETISERS
include olives, bowls (left to
right) of *Taramosalata*
(smooth fish roe dip),
Melitzanosalata (aubergine
purée with garlic) and
Hummus bi tahina
(chick-pea and sesame
paste). In the foreground
are *Loukanika horiatika*,
sausages

SOUPS

Popular throughout the Balkans and regarded as the Greek national soup, *Soupa Avgolemono* is a staple item on any menu. Traditionally it is made with rich chicken stock cooked with rice and thickened with beaten eggs and lemon juice. Fish soups figure prominently, and indeed the Greeks claim that *Kaccavia*, of ancient origin, is *the* original fish soup later purloined by the French as *bouillabaisse*. Other specialities are chunky, anise-flavoured cabbage soup (*lahana*), lentil soups and the traditional Easter soup, *Mayieritsa*, cooked on the entrails and offal of the Easter lamb.

GREEK SOUPS: *Revithio* (chick-pea, onions and lemon) above *Kaccavia* and (right) *Fassolatha* (dried beans and vegetables), sometimes served with *renges*, next to *Soupa Avgolemono*

RICE AND PASTA DISHES

Classical Greece was the cradle of civilization, the birthplace of the culinary arts and the inspiration of Roman gastronomy on which the French *haute cuisine* is founded. As a seafaring and warring nation, Greece was exposed to many foreign influences, and it is hardly surprising that rice pilaf, the national dish of Turkey, and pasta, Italy's staple food, should have been absorbed into the Greek kitchen. All the more so when Greece herself produces in abundance those very ingredients which have a natural affinity with rice and pasta – olive oil, tomatoes, aubergines, garlic, and aromatic herbs.

Makaroni me kreas (opposite)
MACARONI WITH LAMB AND TOMATO SAUCE.
Sometimes spaghetti, noodles or rice are used instead of macaroni

Mithia pilafi (below)
RISOTTO WITH MUSSELS
cooked in olive oil and white wine; garnished with watercress

SAVOURIES AND SNACKS

Orektika
SAVOURY SNACKS
often include a plate
heaped with hot or cold

dolmathes, a pan of sizzling
kokoretsi and a bowl of
refreshing *tzatziki*, a salad
of grated cucumber dressed

Tavernas, coffee houses and street vendors display an array of snacks and savoury dishes, more substantial than *mezethes* though equally good with a bottle of local wine. There are small crisp-fried pastry envelopes stuffed with cottage cheese, minced meat or spinach and known as *Bourekia*; garlic-flavoured pork sausages (*Kokoretsi*) and filling omelettes with potatoes, onion and cheese (*Omeletta me patates*). Above all there are *Dolmathes*, those delicious parcels of vine leaves rolled round a filling of minced meat and/or rice, with currants and herbs.

with garlicky yoghourt; in some parts of Greece this salad is served as a chilled soup. In the background, bowls with mixed nuts, raisins and roasted water-melon seeds

FISH AND SHELLFISH

Offshore fishing is a major industry in Greece, and every morning small fishing boats land the night's catches of sea bass and mullet, skate, octopus and squid, lobsters, prawns, crabs and mussels; from the depths of the Aegean Sea come tunny fish, shoals of sardines and red snappers. A favourite cooking method is *plaki*, a term applied to any fish which is baked or braised with vegetables. Lemon invariably flavours fish – and most other food in Greece, where lemon orchards compete with olive groves. Tomatoes are never combined with lemon though often with baked fish (*Psari fournou*).

1   2

1 Astako
BOILED LOBSTER
In reality, the
Mediterranean spiny
lobster or crawfish, served
hot or cold with a garnish
of tomatoes and olives;
dressed with oil and lemon
juice or with mayonnaise
(*Astako vrastos me
mayonnaisa*)

2 Palamitha plaki
BRAISED BONITO
with celery, tomatoes,
onions, garlic and herbs.
Bonito or palamid is
related to tunny fish and
caught extensively in Greek
waters. Also pickled and
smoked, cut into thin strips
and served as *mezethes*

3

4

3 Barbounia tiyanita
FRIED RED MULLET
marinated with lemon juice
and fried in oil. Classic
Greek dish

4 Kalamarakia tiyanita
DEEP-FRIED BABY SQUID
served hot with lemon
quarters, as *mezethes* or
bought from street vendors

5 Ktapothi krassato
OCTOPUS BRAISED IN RED
WINE
and olive oil, with onions
and herbs

6 Kalamaria yemista
BAKED SQUID
marinated in oil and lemon
juice and stuffed with rice,
onions and pine kernels

5

6

POULTRY AND GAME

Most game dishes are confined to mountain hare and rabbit, which are rarely hung for long before they are made into casseroles with herbs and wine. Partridges and other small game birds also appear on menus, at their most delicious when grilled over a charcoal fire. Mountain kid and goat, so closely associated with Greek mythology, often take the place of lamb and mutton, but are also cooked like game or spit-roasted whole. Chicken is popular, roasted or steamed, in casseroles and *phyllo* pies. Both goose (*hina*) and turkey (*yallopoulo*) come stuffed with chestnuts.

1 Perthikes me elies ke selino
   BRAISED PARTRIDGE WITH
   OLIVES, CELERY AND
   TOMATOES,
   served in the sauce

2 Kotopoulo riyanato
   ROAST CHICKEN FLAVOURED
   WITH WILD OREGANO AND
   LEMON,
   cooked and basted with
   olive oil and butter and
   served with the pan juices

3 Kotopoulo lemonato
   CHICKEN STUFFED WITH
   LEMON
   poached with vegetables,
   jointed and garnished with
   fresh lemon slices; served
   with a rich cream, egg,
   lemon and wine sauce

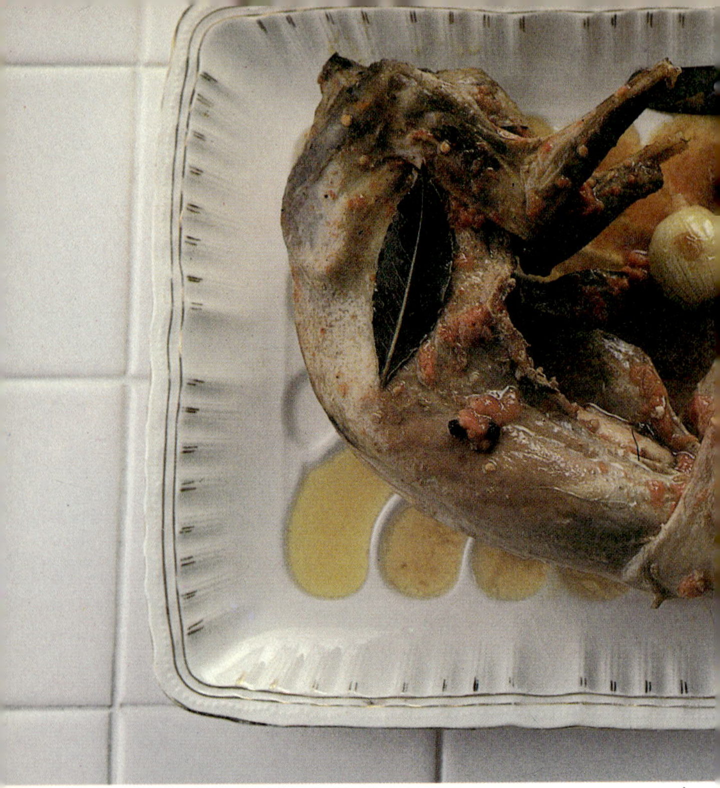

4

5

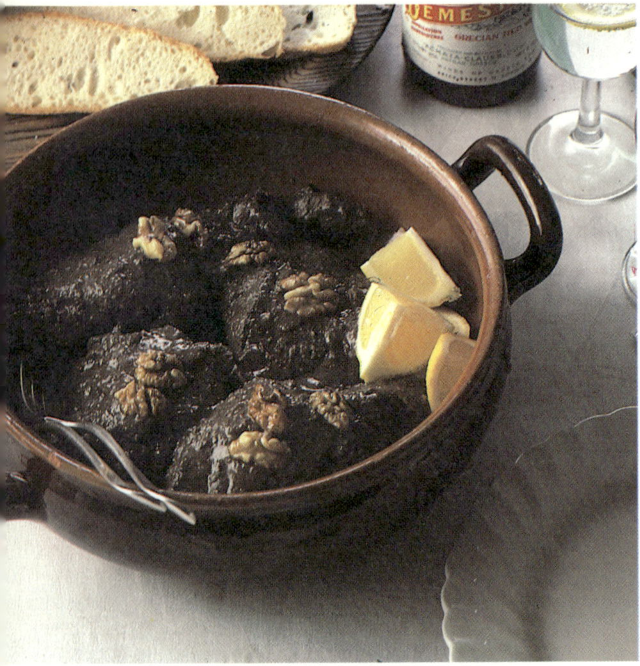

4 Kouneli stifatho (*above*)
RABBIT RAGOÛT
well flavoured with garlic
and spices; cooked with
baby onions, tomato sauce
and wine. Served plainly,
with bread and wine

5 Layos me saltsa karithia
(*far left*)
CASSEROLE OF HARE WITH
WALNUTS
cooked in oil, lemon juice
and brandy, thickened with
ground walnuts. Garnished
with walnut halves and
served on slices of fried
bread

6 Katsikaki psito
WHOLE SPIT-ROASTED KID
seasoned with lemon, garlic
and herbs. Served with the
basting juices or a spicy
wine sauce

MEAT

To the Greeks, meat means lamb and for perfection lamb means a spit-roast. In country districts the spit is still placed over an open trench and slowly turned over hot charcoals, often of pine, which imparts a special tang to the meat. Just as popular are lamb kebabs (*Arni souvlakia*) and the 'turning' kebab (*Dönner kebab*), a Turkish speciality adopted throughout the Balkans: long strips of lamb, marinated with garlic and herbs, are wound round a rotating vertical spit suspended over a charcoal fire. As the meat cooks from the outside, it is carved off in thin slices and served with onions.

1

2

4

1 Mousakas
MEAT AND AUBERGINE PIE

2 Arni exochico (kleftiko)
LAMB IN PARCHMENT CASES

3 Arni kolokithia
CUBED LAMB & COURGETTES

4 Vothino stifatho
BEEF AND ONION STEW

5 Soudzoukakia
MEAT RISSOLES

6 Arni me spanaki
avgolemono
BRAISED LAMB & SPINACH IN
EGG AND LEMON SAUCE

7 Sikotakia me saltsa
(*overleaf*)
CALF'S LIVER IN RED WINE

3

5

6

8 Souvlakia
SPICED LAMB KEBABS
marinated in olive oil and
lemon juice, grilled over
charcoal and served with
side dishes of lemon and
tomato quarters, cucumber,
lettuce, cheese and olives

9 Hirino me selinorizes
BRAISED PORK AND CELERY
in wine with egg and lemon
sauce (*avgolemono*)

10 Moscari kapama
BRAISED VEAL WITH ONIONS,
garlic, herbs and red wine,
often with chopped
tomatoes

8   9

10

VEGETABLES

Haricot beans, aubergines and cabbage are among the most popular vegetables, as accompaniments to main dishes or as separate courses. They are nearly always cooked in combination with other vegetables and with chopped herbs, like the classic *Fassolia* of dried haricot beans cooked with onions, carrots and celery. Cabbage and vine leaves are stuffed with a spicy rice and tomato mixture (*Dolmathes lahana*), and aubergines, artichokes, tomatoes, squashes and peppers are filled with similar stuffings. *Koloki-thopita*, of Greek-American origin, is a baked pie of vegetable marrow layered with onions and tomatoes.

1

1 Melitzanes yemistes
STUFFED AUBERGINES
with onions, tomatoes,
garlic and parsley sautéed
in oil. Served hot

2 Bamies me domates
BRAISED OKRA (LADIES'
FINGERS),
with tomatoes, onions,
garlic and herbs

3 Fassolakia me domates
FRENCH BEANS
sautéed and braised with
onions, tomatoes, sugar
and parsley. Usually served
as a course on its own

4

6

5

4 Spanakopita
SPINACH PIE
of sautéed spinach with
onions, herbs and feta
cheese in thin *phyllo* pastry.
Cut into squares and served
hot or cold

5 Fassolia yiyandes plaki
BUTTER BEANS
sautéed with finely chopped
tomatoes and onions;
sweetened with sugar and
flavoured with mint

6 Anginares a la polita
WHOLE BRAISED ARTICHOKES
cooked in oil and lemon
juice, with carrots, button
onions, new potatoes and
dill; served in the thickened
sauce

SALADS

The mixed green salad is less popular than various cooked or fresh vegetables dressed with chopped herbs and oil or with the traditional *Skorthalia* or garlic sauce. Many preparations termed salads (*salates*) are in fact smooth purées, such as *Melitzanosalata* (aubergines) and the famous *Taramosalata* of pounded fish roe, both of which are served as *mezethes*. Green salads of young dandelion leaves (*rathikia*), French beans (*fassolakia*) and cooked spinach (*spanaki*) are tossed in oil and lemon juice, and tomatoes are stuffed with shrimps.

Salates
SALADS

The so-called Greek salad *Horiatiki salata* is properly an assortment of tit-bits, with oil and lemon juice, for enjoying with drinks: tomatoes, cucumber, onion and pepper rings, sometimes spinach or other salad greens, and always black olives and cubes of feta cheese

Fassolia salata is found on most menus; it consists of cooked butter beans dressed with olive oil, onions and chopped herbs

Marulosalata, a plain green salad of lettuce, spring onions and cucumber is seasoned with lemon only

CHEESES

Greek cheeses, clockwise:
Anari: blue goat's or ewe's
milk cheese. *Halorini*: ewe's

Most Greek cheeses are made from ewe's or goat's milk. The latter has a higher Vitamin B and a lower fat content than cow's milk. Cheeses are generally soft and made locally for local consumption, though some, especially feta, are commercially made for export. Local feta cheese, from the mountains near Athens, is made from ewe's milk; it is pure white, crumbly and extremely salty. There is a blue feta (*Kopanisti*), of finer texture and with a peppery tang. Cottage cheeses are consumed in quantity and used, with honey and sugar, in sweet pies.

milk cheese, flavoured with coriander. *Feta*: white, soft and salty cheese for eating and cooking. *Kefalotyri*: hard and salty cheese, used in cooking

SWEETS AND PASTRIES

It is a well-known fact that the Greeks relish sugary sweet and sticky pastries and cakes. A meal is usually finished with fruit rather than a dessert, but sweet concoctions are consumed in large quantities at coffee and pastry shops. This predilection for sweet things is a typical trait of the Balkan countries, all of which favour excessively sweet honey syrups in which to steep their pastries and ubiquitous *halvas* or semolina cakes. There are deep-fried batter puffs and fritters, served with hot honey sauce, sweet brandy-flavoured chestnut cream and toffees of honey and sesame seeds known as *Pastelli*.

1

1 Baklava
WALNUT PASTRY SOAKED IN
HONEY SYRUP

2 Yaourtopita
YOGHOURT CAKE

3 Karithopita
WALNUT CAKE STEEPED IN
BRANDY SYRUP

Greek pastries (overleaf)
Top right-hand corner:
Koulouria, reminiscent of
Danish pastries, flavoured
with sesame, vanilla, orange
or lemon rind. Far left:
Kourabiethes: (shortbread)
and below *Shamali* (small
phyllo pastries, top),
baklavas and *Amygthalota*,
marzipan pears

FRUIT

A bowl or plate of fresh fruit, perhaps with cubes of fresh or fried feta cheese, is the logical conclusion to a Greek meal. There will, in season, be luscious black and green grapes, juicy water melons, sun-ripened apricots and peaches, purple and green figs, pears from the island of Hydra, and cherries and small sweet strawberries. The fruit which is not eaten fresh is made into jams, jellies and preserves; small bitter oranges and lemons are cooked in heavy syrups, almost like crystallized fruits, and the blossom of tangerines, oranges, lemons and scented roses are made into unusual, delicious jams.

1

1 Fresh fruit,
much of it grown on the sunny islands which dot the Greek Archipelago, is always in evidence. With coarse black bread, olives and local cheese, fresh fruit constitutes many a tasty lunch

2 Ylyka koutaliou
Literally SPOON SWEETS, preserves of figs, oranges, pears and cherries are traditionally offered in small bowls, with spoons and glasses of liqueurs as the ancient symbols of hospitality

WINES

Like many other pleasures of the table, wine has been produced and enjoyed in Greece since ancient times. The god of wine, Dionysus, his brow adorned with a wreath of vine leaves, was worshipped and offered sacrifices from the grape harvest. While the Anglo-Saxons broke their fast with bitter ale in the morning, the Greeks contentedly dunked their bread in oil and wine. Commercially, Greece has lagged behind other wine-producing countries, but there are still good wines to be had – red, rosé or white, sweet or dry. Retsina, the most familiar and redolent of pine resin, is perhaps an acquired taste.

Greek red wines, commonly labelled *Mavros*, include table wines such as Demestica, the dry Castel Danielis types, akin to Burgundy and in the expensive price range, and various light rosé wines (*Kokkineli*). Mavrodaphne, a sweet wine, is considered the best red

White wines are generally dry and light; they range from Retsinas of various qualities to Demestica, Santa Laura and Santa Helena, all pleasant and undemanding. The sweet white muscat wines from Samos have a character entirely their own

COFFEE AND LIQUEURS

Coffee houses (*kafenion*) are as typically Greek as *tavernas* and *bouzoukia* music, yet the preparation and presentation of coffee are of Turkish origin. There are certain rigidly observed ceremonies attached to after-dinner coffee, ranging from *sketto* (without sugar) to *metrio* (medium sweet). Very sweet Turkish coffee is *variyliki*. Traditionally, coffee is poured from a long-handled copper or brass pot, served with glasses of water and the inevitable bowl of Turkish delight (*Rahat lokum*) – and sometimes roasted cardamom seeds.

The Greek spirit is *ouzo*, a clear fiery liquid distilled from grapes. It is taken as an aperitif, with water when it becomes cloudy, like Pernod. Seasoned drinkers take *ouzo* neat, with a plate of *mezethes.* The best known liqueur brandies are the Metaxa brands

GLOSSARY OF GREEK MENU AND CULINARY TERMS

A

Achini: sea-urchins, served raw with lemon juice and bread as appetiser.

Agrafa: type of Gruyère cheese made from ewe's milk.

Ajem pilaf: meat or poultry pilaf with onions and herbs.

Akhlathi: pear.

> **À la Grecque** is a French culinary term describing a pickling method for vegetables such as artichokes, mushrooms, button onions and leeks. The method has been adopted from the Greek cuisine, where it is known as *a la polita*, acknowledging its origin to Constantinople. Many Greek dishes show strong influences from the neighbouring Balkan countries, Turkey and Italy, or *vice versa*, for the national cuisines of Europe and the Middle East are all founded on the culinary arts of ancient Greece.

Alati: salt.

Alverof: see Faki me pasta.

Amygthala: almonds.

Amygthalota: almond paste, shaped like pears, baked and dusted with icing sugar.

Anari: salty, round or square mottled cheese from goat's or ewe's milk.

Andithia: chicory.
  avgolémono: braised in butter and lemon juice; served with egg and lemon sauce.

Anginares: globe artichokes.
  a la polita: cooked whole in olive oil and lemon juice with new potatoes, onions, carrots, salad onions and dill; served in the sauce. Cooking method known in classic cuisine as *à la grecque* and in Greece as the Constantinople style.
  me koykia: artichoke bottoms and fresh broad beans in white sauce with olive oil, lemon juice and parsley.
  tiyanites: whole boiled artichokes, dipped in egg and breadcrumbs and deep-fried.
  vrastes: whole boiled artichokes.
  yemistes: broad beans and artichokes stuffed with onion, garlic, celery and herbs.

Angouria: cucumber.
  yemista: stuffed with diced shellfish or feta cheese.

Antholyti: round, pale yellow cheese with thick and wrinkled rind.

Anthotyro: firm and mild goat cheese from Crete; eaten with grapes.

Aravosito: sweet corn.

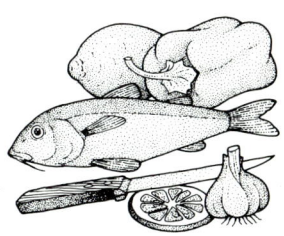

Arnaki: young lamb or kid.
sti souvla: milk-fed lamb
charcoal-grilled with broad
beans, onions and garlic;
traditional at Easter.
yemisto: roasted whole,
stuffed with the minced offal,
onions, rice, mint and
cinnamon.

Arni: lamb.
exochico: flavoured with
garlic and herbs; baked in
parchment cases.
fricasse avgolémono: stew
with onion, lettuce and herbs
in egg and lemon sauce.
kokkinisto me bamies: lamb
and okra braised in tomato
sauce.
me domates: braised lamb
with tomatoes; served with
rice or pasta.
me fassolia fresca: braised
with sautéed French beans,
tomatoes, onions and garlic.
me kolokithia: lamb stew
with courgettes and
tomatoes.
me maroulia: stew with
lettuce hearts, onions and
dill.
me spageto: lamb cooked
with spaghetti and tomatoes.
me spanaki avgolémono:
stewed lamb served with
spinach and egg and lemon
sauce.
psito: roast lamb flavoured
with garlic.
souvlakia: spicy lamb
kebabs.
sto fourno horiatiko: lamb

baked with feta cheese and
tomatoes.

Arnissia payithakia riyanata:
lamb cutlets with marjoram
sauce.

Aspro: white (of wine).

Astako: spiny lobster or
crawfish, often served hot
cooked in a thick sauce of
onion, tomatoes, white wine
and oil, with seasoning. Cold,
it is dressed with oil and
lemon juice.
mayioneza: served cold with
mayonnaise.

Avgo: eggs
me domates ke kremithia:
scrambled eggs topped with
sautéed tomatoes and onions.

Avgolémono, saltsa: fluffy
sauce of egg yolks beaten
with lemon juice; traditional
Greek sauce served with
meat, fish, poultry and
vegetable dishes, or added to
soups, casseroles and stews.

Avgotaraho: grey mullet roe,
the basic ingredient in
taramosalata. Also called
botargo and red caviar.

B

Bakalaos (Bakaliaros): salted
cod, usually cooked Plaki.
skorthalia: cod coated with
batter and deep-fried; served
with garlic (*skorthalia*) sauce.
vrastos: boiled salted cod
with onions, celery and
potatoes; served with oil and

lemon juice dressing.

Baklavas: sweet pastries filled with chopped walnuts and almonds; coated with honey syrup.

Bamies: okra.
me domates: okra fried with onions, tomatoes and parsley. Served as separate course.

Barbounia: red mullet.
savore: cooked in white wine, tomato sauce, garlic and rosemary. Served cold.
sti schara: grilled and served with lemon juice and olive oil.
sto harti: mullet baked with herbs in parchment cases.
tiyanita: fried mullet, seasoned with lemon; extremely popular dish.

Becatses: woodcock.

Bira: beer.

Botargo: see Avgotaraho.

Bourekia: Phyllo patties with savoury fillings (minced meat, cream cheese or spinach). Fried and served as appetiser. Also called bourekakia.

Bourtheto: baked white fish with onions and tomatoes; fiery hot with cayenne pepper.

Brizola: cutlet, chop.

C

Composta: fruit compôte.
milo: apple compôte.

Crema: cornflour sweet, flavoured with orange or tangerine peel and vanilla essence; served chilled decorated with chopped nuts.

Christopsomo is the Greek Christmas bread traditional at the Feast of the Epiphany on January 6. The soft yeast loaf is flavoured with orange peel and sesame seeds, decorated with a dough cross and topped with finely chopped nuts. Special shortbread biscuits (*kourabiethes*) are also baked for Christmas and the New Year. They are flavoured with ouzo and decorated with whole cloves as symbols of the spices brought from the East by the Three Wise Men.

D

Diosmos: mint.

Diples: sweet pasty soaked in honey syrup.

Dolmathakia: small version of dolmathe.

Dolmathes: vine leaves stuffed with savoury, often rice, filling. Braised in lemon and tomato-flavoured stock, served hot with yoghourt sauce or cold on their own.

lahana: cabbage leaves stuffed with garlic-flavoured rice, pine kernels, sultanas and tomatoes; served hot with tomato and cream sauce.

Domates: tomatoes.
yemistes: baked tomatoes stuffed with rice, onion, currants, pine kernels, parsley, mint and garlic.
yemistes me kima: baked, stuffed with minced meat and onions.
yemistes me melitzanes: stuffed with cheese-flavoured aubergine and tomato pulp.
yemistes me yarithes: fresh, peeled tomatoes stuffed with shrimps and mayonnaise.
saltsa domates: tomato sauce flavoured with garlic and onion, and sometimes with ginger and nutmeg.

Donner kebab: thin lamb slices, strongly flavoured with garlic and herbs, wound round a vertical revolving spit and grilled on charcoal.

Drakena: Mediterranean saltwater fish (dragon-fish), similar to whiting.

E

Elies: olives. Invaluable in Greek cooking; both black and green olives are pickled in brine and added to every kind of savoury dish.

Eleolatho: olive oil.

Enkephalos: brains.

Entrathes: main dishes (on a menu).

Entrathia: pot roast, usually beef, with vegetables.

F

Faki: brown lentils.
me pasta: cooked lentils and noodles garnished with fried onions. Also known as Alverof.

Fangri: sea-bream.

Fassolakia: beans.
freska: French or runner beans, often cooked in oil.
me domates: cooked in oil with tomatoes and parsley.
salata: French bean salad dressed with olive oil and lemon juice.

Fassolatha: National dish of dried bean soup cooked with celery, carrots and onions in olive oil, tomato purée and herb-flavoured stock.

Fassolia: dried haricot or butter beans.
me hirino: haricot beans, diced pork and onions cooked in tomato sauce.
salata: cooked haricot beans, dressed with oil, chopped onions and parsley.
yahni: cooked with carrots, onions and celery in oil and tomato purée.
yiachni: fried haricot beans, cooked with garlic, thyme and tomato purée; garnished

with raw onion rings and served hot as a separate course.

yiyandes plaki: cooked in oil with chopped onions, tomatoes, garlic and mint.

Fava: yellow split peas, boiled and served cold as a salad purée dressed with olive oil, lemon juice and chopped onions.

Feta: popular curd cheese from ewe's milk ; pure white, soft and salty.

Finikia: small brandy-flavoured honey cakes garnished with sesame seeds. Also called Melomakarona.

Fithés: vermicelli pasta.

Floyeres: pastry rolls with almond filling, coated with syrup.

Fournou: baked.

Frape: iced, chilled.

Fruta: fruit.

Fystikia: pistachio nuts.

G, H

Graviera: Gruyère type of cheese made from ewe's milk. Cretan speciality.

Halorini: ewe's milk cheese flavoured with coriander.

Halumi: soft cheese, similar to feta, but less salty.

Halvas: cinnamon-flavoured semolina and almond cake soaked in lemon juice.

toufournou: similar, but lighter from the addition of

eggs; both cake and syrup flavoured with brandy. Also known as *Halvas tis Rinas*.

Hanoi: small pink fish, used in soups.

Imam bayildi can be found on most taverna menus and is acclaimed as a Greek speciality, although it originated in Turkey, *Imam* being the Turkish word for priest. The literal translation is 'the fainting Imam' an epithet with various explanations, ranging from the Imam's delight at the dish to his collapse after over-indulgence and to his anguish at the cost of the rich ingredients. Certainly the three stories can all be accounted for, considering the large amount of olive oil in which a tomato, onion and garlic mixture is cooked. This is then stuffed into aubergines, which are baked in a pool of oil and left to get cold.

Hilopites me kima: minced lamb with onions, garlic and tomatoes, mixed with cooked noodles.

Hina: goose.

yemisti: roast goose stuffed with chestnuts, apples and

pine kernels.

Hirines: pork chops

Hirino: pork.
 brizoles krassata: pork chops
 in red wine.
 me selinorizes: braised in red
 wine with celery, onions,
 herbs and avgolémono sauce.
 psito: spit-roasted sucking
 pig.

Horiatiki: mixed salad of
 tomatoes, onions, cucumber,
 peppers and feta cheese.

Horta: collective term for salad
 vegetables.

Htapothi: octopus.
 krassato: octopus cooked in
 red wine and olive oil with
 onions and garlic; served
 with rice.
 stiffatho me kremithia: stew
 of young octopus in white
 wine with tomato purée,
 onions and garlic.

K

Kaccania (kakavia); fish soup
 cum stew with white wine,
 garlic, tomatoes and
 vegetables; served with
 croûtons. Similar to French
 bouillabaisse.

Kafes: Turkish coffee.
 mavros: black coffee,
 whether Turkish or
 continental.

Kaïmaki: thick cream.

Kalamarakia: baby squid,
 usually deep-fried in oil,
 plain or coated with batter.

Served as appetiser.

Kalamaria: squid.
 yemista: squid stuffed with
 rice, onions, parsley, dill and
 pine kernels, baked in oil, red
 wine and tomato juice and
 served cold.

Karaoli: snails.

Kafenion are to the Greeks
what cafés are to the
Venetians – popular
meeting places for lengthy
discussions of domestic
and international affairs
over endless cups of coffee.
In Greece, the coffee is of
the Turkish variety,
poured from a long-
handled brass pot into tiny
cups and served with
glasses of water to wash
down the inevitable coffee
grounds. There are certain
inflexible rules to be
followed when ordering
Turkish coffee or *kafes*,
which is boiled with (or
without) sugar according
to the order. Coffee
without sugar is *sketto*
while *me oliyi* has a trace
of sugar; *metrio* is
medium sweet, and *mallo
yliki* rather sweet. *Yliki* is
sweet coffee, and *variyliki*
is very sweet. Add *vrasto*
to the coffee of your
choice, and it will come
without cream.

Karithia: walnuts.
Karithopita: walnut cake soaked in brandy-flavoured syrup. Speciality of Athens.
Karpouzi: water-melon.
Karveli: soft wheat bread.
Kasseri: firm white cheese used grated in cooking.
Kastana: chestnuts.
  purée: dessert of sieved chestnuts, topped with whipped cream.
Kataifi: thin pastry strips shaped as small diamond parcels with a filling of chopped almonds and butter; soaked in lemon syrup.
Katsikaki: kid.
  psito: whole roasted kid.
Kataloyos: menu.
Kefalotyri: hard, salty cheese, resembling Parmesan; used in cooking.
Keftethakia: tiny meat dumplings.
Keftethes: meat rissoles with mint and parsley.
  tarano: small rissoles of grey mullet or cod roe, flavoured with onions and herbs and deep-fried.
Kephalos: grey mullet.
Khtapothi: octopus.
Kima: mince meat sauce for pasta.
Kiniyi: collective term for game.
Kokkino: red.
Kokoretsi: spiced lamb sausage; spit-roasted and basted with oil and lemon juice.
Kolokassi: sweet potatoes.
Kolokithakia: vegetable marrow or squash.
  yiachni: squash cooked in oil with onions, tomatoes and parsley; served with grated cheese.
Kolokithia: courgettes.
  yemista: courgettes stuffed with meat and rice; baked in tomato sauce.
Kolokithokeftethes: fried marrow and cheese rissoles.
Kolokithopita: baked marrow layered with tomatoes, onions and herbs.
Kopanisti: blue feta cheese, fine-textured and with peppery flavour.
Kotopita: phyllo pie with boned chicken, onion purée and cheese.
Kotopoulo: chicken.
  bamies: chicken casserole with tomato purée and okra.
  hilopites: chicken braised in white wine, with onions, garlic, celery and tomatoes; served with noodles.
  kapama: chicken in spicy tomato sauce.
  riyanato: roast chicken with marjoram.
  sti stamma: chicken cooked in earthenware pot, with wine, tomato purée and herbs.
  tis scharas: spit-roasted chicken served with oil and lemon juice or garlic (skorthalia) sauce.
Kotosoupa: chicken soup.

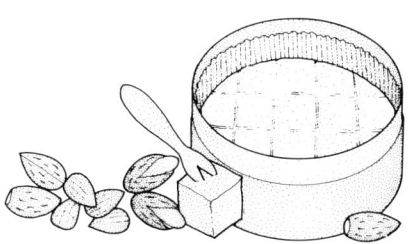

Koukia: dried broad beans.
  freska: fresh broad beans.
Koukla: small deep-fried meat
  rissoles.
Koulouria: sweet bread, shaped
  like rings or rolls, sprinkled
  with sesame seeds.
Kouneli: rabbit.
  me kaïmaki: rabbit casserole
  with cream.
  riyanato: roast rabbit
  flavoured with marjoram,
  garlic and lemon.
  stifatho: rabbit stew with
  onions and garlic in tomato
  and onion sauce.
Koupepia: stuffed vegetable
  marrow.
Kourabiethes: shortbread
  biscuits, traditional at
  Christmas and New Year.
  me amygthalo: with chopped
  almonds in the dough.
Krasata: squid cooked in oil
  and red wine, with tomatoes
  and herbs.
Krasi: wine.
Kreas: meat.
  ke lahanika sti catsarola: beef
  casserole with red and white
  cabbage, potatoes, tomatoes,
  green peppers, dried beans,
  onions and white wine.
  me elies: beef or veal in
  tomato sauce with pickled
  green olives.
  me kastana: beef or veal
  cooked with chestnuts and
  onions.
  me kythonia: lamb, beef or
  veal braised with quinces and
  onions.

Kreatopita: rich shortcrust pie,
  with lamb, kid or goat, and
  chicken, onions, tomatoes,
  rice, grated cheese, raisins,
  white wine and garlic.
Krema karamele: cream
  caramel.
Kremithakia: button onions.
  freska: salad onions.
Kremithia: onions.
Krio: cold.
Kritharaki: fine barley used to
  thicken soups and stews.
Kythonia: quinces, often served
  or cooked with meat. Also
  sea quinces, small shellfish
  sold by street vendors and
  eaten raw like Achini.

L

Lahana: cabbage.
  dolmathes me hirino: cabbage
  leaves stuffed with minced
  meat and rice; served with
  avgolémono sauce.
  yiachni: braised in oil with
  onions, celery, tomatoes and
  capers.
Lahaniká: collective term for
  vegetables.
Lakertha: pickled smoked
  tunny, swordfish or bonito;
  served as appetiser.
Lambropsomo: yeast-raised
  Easter bread with orange
  peel and sesame seeds,
  decorated with four scarlet
  eggs (*kokkina avga*).
Latheres: applied to food
  braised in olive oil.

Latholémono: creamy sauce of olive oil and lemon juice.

Lathoxitho: salad dressing of olive oil, lemon juice (or vinegar), mustard and seasoning.

Lavraki: fish baked with butter, cream and lemon juice.

Layos: hare.
me saltsa: casserole of hare in white wine and brandy sauce.
me saltsa karithia: similar, with the addition of walnuts.
stifatho: hare stew with onions, garlic, currants and tomato sauce.

Lemoni: lemon.

Lithrini: sea bass.

Loukanika: pork and beef sausage flavoured with garlic, cinnamon, orange peel and peppercorns; served as hot appetiser.

Loukoumathes: yoghourt fritters, deep-fried and soaked in honey syrup.

Loukoumi: type of Turkish delight, with almonds or pistachio nuts.

Lounza: cured pork fillet, served raw, in thin slices, as an appetiser.

Loyariasmos: bill.

M

Makaronatha: macaroni with meat sauce.

Makaroni: collective term for pasta.
me kima: spaghetti with meat sauce.
me saltsa domata: spaghetti with tomato sauce.

Manouri: mild, soft ewe's milk cheese.

Manti: pasty filled with minced meat and onions; soaked in chicken broth.

Marithes: deep-fried whitebait.

Mayieritsa: tripe soup, with rice and egg and lemon sauce; traditional on Easter Sunday.

Mayioneza: mayonnaise.

Melachrino: spiced Easter cake.
xantho: layer cake sandwiched with meringue mixed with chopped nuts.

Meli: honey.

Melitzanes: aubergines.
papoutsakia: baked aubergines stuffed with minced meat, covered with béchamel sauce and grated cheese.
salata: garlic-flavoured aubergine purée with oil and lemon juice; served cold as a salad dip.
tiyanites: aubergine fritters.
yahni: aubergine slices sautéed with onions, tomatoes, garlic and herbs.
yemistes: baked aubergines stuffed with tomato, onions and garlic. Modified version of Imam bayildi.

Melomakarona: see Finikia.

Melopita: sweet pastry flan

with a filling of honey, eggs and cottage cheese.

Mezethes: appetisers, with drinks. Also called mezethakia.

Miala: brains.
  salata: cold salad of cooked lamb's brains dressed with olive oil and lemon juice.

Milo: apple.

Mithia (mythia): mussels.
  pilafi: mussels with rice, onions and tomato sauce.
  tiyanita: sautéed mussels with garlic and tomato sauce.
  yemista: mussels in the shell stuffed with rice, pine kernels, onions and currants; cooked in tomato purée and wine.

Moscari: veal.
  kapama: veal braised in red wine with garlic, tomatoes and herbs.
  psito sto fournou: pot-roasted veal with tomatoes, onions and garlic.
  stifatho: veal, onion and tomato râgout in red wine.

Mousakas: national dish of Greece, with numerous variations. Typically, it consists of layers of sautéed aubergines, minced lamb or beef with onions, tomatoes, herbs and spices, topped with béchamel sauce and baked.

Moustartha: mustard.
  saltsa: garlic-flavoured sauce of mustard, olive oil and lemon juice.

Mythia: see mithia.

Myzithra: soft cottage cheese, a by-product from the making of feta cheese.

N

Nefra: kidneys.
Nerantzi: bitter oranges.
  yiristo: orange peel preserve.
Nero: water.
Nerole: orange-flower water.

O

Omeletta: omelette.
  me patates: sautéed potatoes and onions in cheese-flavoured omelette mixture; served flat not folded.
  me rizi: egg and rice omelette garnished with tomato slices coated with breadcrumbs and sautéed.

Ostreon: oysters.

P

Pagithakia: lamb chops.
  hasapika: lamb chops baked with onions, tomatoes, herbs and new potatoes.

Palamitha: bonito.
  plaki: bonito braised with vegetables, tomatoes and garlic.
  sto harti: bonito baked in paper cases.

Papia: duck.
Papoutsakia: baked stuffed

aubergines with béchamel sauce and grated cheese. See also Melitzanes.

Parnossus: white ewe's milk cheese.

Passa tempo: hot roasted nuts, water-melon and sunflower seeds and hot savouries sold by street vendors.

Pasta ke faki: boiled noodles and lentils garnished with fried onions.

Pastakithona: small squares of quince and almond paste, sold at confectioners and pastry shops.

Pasta makarouna: dish of minced meat and pasta, arranged in layers with grated cheese, and baked.

Pastelli: type of soft toffee made from honey and sesame seeds.

Pastitsio: popular dish of meat ragoût layered with macaroni (or noodles), cream sauces and grated cheese.

Pastourmá: smoked, strongly garlic-flavoured bacon, served as appetiser.

Patátes: potatoes.
keftethes: fried potato cakes with onions, tomatoes and herbs.
kroketes: potato croquettes coated with grated cheese and deep-fried; often served as appetiser.
purée me kreas: similar to English shepherd's pie.
yiachni: potatoes sautéed in oil with onions and tomatoes.

Patsia: tripe and pig's trotter soup to which avgolémono sauce is added.

Payoto: ice cream, usually made from ewe's milk.

Peinirlis: bread rolls filled with meat, eggs or cheese.

Peponi: melon.

Perthikes: partridge.
me elies ke selino: partridge braised with celery, olives and tomatoes.

Phyllo requires the kind of dexterity which only years of practice can bring, and most of this Greek speciality is bought from professional pastry cooks. The dough is easy enough – plain flour and water – but it is kneaded and twirled and rolled and stretched until it is paper thin. Phyllo pastry is used for savoury pies such as spinach pie (*spanakopita*) and chicken pie (*kotopita*), as well as for the stickily sweet baklavas and the small almond turnovers known as *floyeres*.

Piaz: salad of cooked dried beans and sliced onions, dressed with olive oil, lemon juice and parsley.

Pihti hirino: pork brawn served as a main course with olive

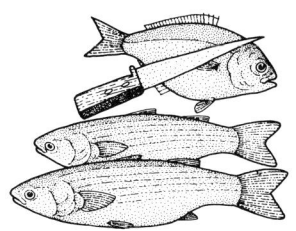

oil and vinegar dressing.

Pilafi: basic rice dish cooked in oil, stock and tomato purée.
me domates: tomato pilaf.
mithia: boiled rice with mussels and onions cooked in oil and white wine.
tou fournou: baked rice with meat, fish, poultry or vegetables.
Greek-American in origin and substantial enough to constitute a main course.
yarithes: fried boiled rice with shrimps, flavoured with marjoram.

Pinthos: hard salty cheese used grated in cooking.

Piperies: sweet peppers.
yemistes: with various savoury stuffings.

Pitta: flat, unleavened bread.

Plaki: method of braising or baking fish with vegetables.

Polita: applied to dishes cooked in the Constantinople style. See also Anginares.

Poulerika: collective term for poultry.

Psaria: fish dishes.

Psari: fish.
fournou: whole fish baked with tomatoes, sometimes with potatoes and onions.
fournou me krassi: baked fish in mustard-flavoured wine sauce.
me rigani: fish grilled with marjoram.
me saltsa kremithia: fish baked in onion sauce with tomatoes and capers.
picti: poached fish served cold in aspic.
plaki me elies: baked fish with black olives, onions, tomatoes and garlic.
psito: charcoal-grilled fish.
spetsiotiko: fish baked in oil and white wine, with tomatoes and garlic; topped with breadcrumbs.
yemisto: baked fish, stuffed with breadcrumbs, onions, celery and shrimps.

Psarosoupa: fish soup, clear or with rice.

Psito: roast (of meat).

Psomi: collective term for bread.

R

Rahat lokum: Turkish delight.

Rathikia: dandelion; popular salad ingredient.

Renga: smoked herring pieces dressed with oil and lemon juice; served as appetiser.

Repanakia: radishes.

Revani: type of sponge cake glazed with lemon syrup.

Revithia: chick-peas, often roasted and salted and served as appetiser or bought from street vendors.
yiachni: chick-peas cooked with onions, tomatoes, garlic and herbs.

Revithiosoupa: chick-pea and onion soup.

Rifaki: kid.

Rigani: wild marjoram.

Ripieno: forcemeat or stuffing.
Rizi: rice.
Rizoyalo: rice pudding, served cold.
Rothakino: peach.
Rouló: meat loaf baked in spicy tomato and red wine sauce; served with noodles.
me makaronia: beef braised with tomatoes.

S

Sadziki: another name for Tzatziki.
Saganaki: fried squares of feta cheese.
Salata: salad. Also cooked, dressed vegetables and purées of fish, meat, chicken, vegetables or pasta.
Salepi: sweet infusion of orchid tubers, sold by street vendors.
Saltsa: sauce. See also avgolémono, domates, latholémono, lathoxitho, mayioneza, moustartha and skorthalia.
Sardeles: sardines.
riganato: fresh sardines baked with olive oil, lemon juice and marjoram.
Sarmathes: cabbage leaves stuffed with meat, rice and onions. See also Lahana.
Scaltsounia: small pastry turnovers filled with ground walnuts and almonds.
Scoubri: mackerel.
plaki: mackerel fillets cooked in olive oil and wine, with onions and tomatoes.
yemista: baked, stuffed with raisins and pine kernels.
Selino: celery.
Selinorrizes: celeriac.
Sfogato: type of soufflé with minced meat and courgettes; served with tomato sauce.
Sika: figs.
Sikotakia: liver.
me saltsa: marinated, fried calf's liver in red wine sauce.
tiganita: liver kebabs sautéed in oil and lemon juice.
tis kottas me saltsa: chicken livers and lamb kidneys cooked in consommé and Madeira wine.
Skaltsounia: deep-fried pastries filled with feta cheese; soaked in honey.
Skembe: tripe.
Skorthalia: classic Greek sauce of crushed garlic pounded with salt, olive oil and lemon juice.
me amygthala: with the addition of ground almonds.
me avgo: with added egg yolks.
me fystikia: with ground pistachio nuts.
me karithia: with ground walnuts.
me patetes: with mashed potatoes.
me yaletta: with breadcrumbs.
Sofrito: fried steaks braised in thick wine sauce strongly flavoured with garlic.
Soudzoukakia: fried veal or

pork sausages; flavoured with garlic and herbs; served with rice and tomato and vermouth sauce.

Soupa: soup.

avgolémono: chicken consommé with rice and egg and lemon sauce.

domato: tomato soup made with fresh tomato juice; served with rice or pasta.

lahana: cabbage and tomato soup.

pasta: clear beef consommé garnished with fine pasta.

trahana: chicken broth with fine pasta made from goat's milk and wheat (*trahana*).

Souvlakia: lamb and vegetable kebabs grilled over charcoal; often sold by street vendors.

Souvlas: spit-roasted.

Spagheto: spaghetti.

me kima saltsa: with sauce of minced beef, onions, tomatoes, garlic, cinnamon and herbs.

Spanaki: spinach.

salata: cooked spinach served cold dressed with oil and lemon juice.

Spanakopita: spinach pie with onions, dill and parsley, and sometimes feta cheese, in phyllo pastry; served hot or cold.

Spanakorizo: spinach cooked in olive oil and water with rice and onions.

Stafili: grapes.

Stiphátho: sautéed.

vothino: beef stew with wine,

tomato purée, onions and garlic.

kotopoulo stiphatho: chicken stew with walnuts and feta cheese.

Storioni: sturgeon.

Synagritha: dentex, a mackerel-like fish.

T

Tallatouri: chilled, garlic-flavoured yoghourt soup with cucumber and walnuts.

The taverna is the centre of social life in Greece, much like a pub in England. It is often small and often no more than a few tables and chairs in a courtyard, but always in the throes of preparing food, Greek food. There are superior and mediocre tavernas, bright or dingy, neither very expensive but all possessed of infinite time and quite incapable of rushing up a meal in a hurry. On the other hand, they hardly ever close, and eating and drinking go on late into the night. Some have *bouzouki* or guitar music, singing and dancing, and tourist-orientated tavernas stage nightly floor shows.

Taramo: fish roe, chiefly from the grey mullet.

Telemes: square, very salty cheese, similar to feta.

Thalasina: shellfish.

Tiganates: smelts.

Tiri: collective term for cheese.

Tiri tiganismeno: another name for Saganaki.

Tiropeta: pie or small pastry with cheese and eggs.

Tis-oras: cooked to order.

Tiyanites: honey and brandy fritters garnished with ground walnuts.

Tonnos: tunny (tuna) fish.

Touloumotyre: large, pure white feta cheese packed in goatskin.

Toursi: pickled, of vegetables and fruit.

Trahana: type of dumpling, made from wheat and goat's milk.
soupa: chicken broth thickened with grated trahana.

Triandafillo yliko: rose petal preserve.

Tsai: tea.

Tsargana: small swordfish.

Tsipoura: snapper; salt-water fish resembling sea bass in taste; usually served grilled.

Tsiri salata: small, dried salted fish, filleted and grilled, then marinated in olive oil and lemon juice; served as an appetiser.

Tsourekia: plaited yeast buns, traditional at Easter.

Tyropita: cheese pie in phyllo pastry.

Tzatziki: cucumber and yoghourt salad or dip with oil and vinegar, flavoured with garlic; often served chilled as a soup.

V

Vasilopita: yeast cake or bread flavoured with sesame seeds and cinnamon; traditional at New Year.

Verikoka: apricots.

Vissinatha: cherry syrup drink, served iced.

Vissino: morello cherry.

Vothinó: beef.
filleto riyanato: grilled steaks flavoured with marjoram and lemon juice.
me lahanika: beef stew with potatoes and vegetables.
stifatho: thick beef stew with white wine, onions, garlic and tomatoes.

Vutiro: butter.

Y

Yala: milk.

Yalaktopolia: small dairy shop or eating place serving yoghourts, chilled rice pudding and crema.

Yalatoboureko: phyllo pie with vanilla-flavoured semolina custard cream; glazed with syrup.

Yaletta: breadcrumbs.

Yallopoulo: turkey.
yemistes: roasted, stuffed with minced lamb, turkey liver, chestnuts, rice, onions, pine kernels and apples.

Yaourti: yoghourt.

Yaourtopita: 1) yoghourt cake. 2) pastry flan filled with honey-flavoured yoghourt and cream cheese.

Yarithes: shrimps.
me saltsa: shrimps served hot in onion and tomato sauce.

Yemissis: stuffing.
horis kreas: onions, rice, pine kernels and parsley.
me kreas ke rizi: meat, rice and herb stuffing for dolmas.
me kreas ke selinor: meat, rice, onion, celery and spice stuffing.
me rizi: rice, onions, tomato purée, currants, pine kernels and herbs.

Yemista: collective term for baked, stuffed vegetables.

Yiachni: braising method which includes onions and olive oil.

Yialandji: collective term for vegetarian dishes.

Yiouvarlakia: meat balls served in avgolémono sauce.

Yiouvetsi: lamb casserole with tomato sauce, noodles, macaroni and cheese.

Ylika: collective term for desserts.

Yliko: fruit preserve.
triandafillo: rose-petal jam, often served at breakfast.

Ylossa: saltwater fish resembling sole.

Yourounaki: sucking pig.
yemisto me feta: roast sucking pig stuffed with feta cheese.

Youvarlakia: poached meat and rice croquettes cooked in egg and lemon sauce.

Z

Zakhari: sugar.

Zesto: hot.

ACKNOWLEDGEMENTS

Photography
All photographs were supplied by the
Anthony Blake Photo Library

Artists
Stonecastle Graphics

The publishers also wish to acknowledge the help given by
La Petite Cuisine
George C. Metaxas
Milia & Co.
Mrs. Rena Salaman-Fokionithou
White Tower Restaurant

Typesetting by MS Filmsetting Limited, Frome, Somerset
Printed in Great Britain by Balding & Mansell, Wisbech, Cambridge